RIDDLES FOR KIDS

Over 300 riddles and Jokes for Children
M. Prefontaine

Published by MP Publishing
Copyright © 2016

What goes up and down stairs without moving?

Answer: Carpet

What can run but never walks, has a mouth but never talks, has a head but never weeps, has a bed but never sleeps?

Answer: A river

What do ghosts eat on Halloween?

Answer: Ghoulash.

Why was six afraid of seven?

Answer: Because seven ate nine.

What's brown and sticky?

Answer: A stick.

What goes up when rain comes down?

Answer: An umbrella

What color socks do bears wear?

Answer: They don't wear socks; they have bear feet.

What type of cheese is made backwards?

Answer: Edam

What happened when a red ship crashed into a blue ship?

Answer: The crew was marooned.

What do ghosts like for dessert?

Answer: I scream.

How do you get straight A's?

Answer: Use a ruler.

I went into the woods and got it, I sat down to seek it, I brought it home with me because I couldn't find it.

Answer: A splinter

What animal keeps the best time?

Answer: A watch dog.

Which case is not a case.

Answer: A staircase

What do you get from a pampered cow?

Answer: Spoiled milk.

Why don't dogs make good dancers?

Answer: Because they have two left feet.

Why was the teacher cross-eyed?

Answer: She couldn't control her pupils.

What to polar bears eat for lunch?

Answer: Ice berg-ers.

Why can't a woman living in the U.S. be buried in Canada?

Answer: Because she's still alive.

That's the worst vegetable to serve on a boat?

Answer: Leeks.

Where do cows go for entertainment?

Answer: To the moo-vies.

What do you find in the middle of nowhere?

Answer: The letter "h".

When is an Irish potato not an Irish potato?

Answer: When it's a French fry.

What do you call a grizzly bear caught in the rain?

Answer: A drizzly bear.

What has hands but cannot clap?

Answer: A clock

Why do you need a license for a dog and not for a cat?

Answer: Cats can't drive.

What room is useless for a ghost?

Answer: A living room.

What would you call the USA if everyone had a pink car?

Answer: A pink carnation.

What would you call the USA if everyone lived in their cars?

Answer: An incarnation.

What did the farmer call the cow that had no milk?

Answer: An udder failure.

What's black and white, black and white, and black and white?

Answer: A panda bear rolling down a hill.

What happened to the lost cattle?

Answer: Nobody's herd.

What do you call doing 2,000 pounds of laundry?

Answer: Washing-ton.

Why do bears have fur coats?

Answer: Because they look silly wearing jackets.

Why can't you shock cows?

Answer: They've herd it all.

If an electric train is travelling south, which way is the smoke going?

Answer: There is no smoke, it's an electric train.

What do you get if you cross a grizzly bear and a harp?

Answer: A bear-faced lyre.

How many months have 28 days?

Answer: All 12 months.

What was T. rex's favorite number?

Answer: Eight

What can fill a room but takes up no space?

Answer: Light

What's the problem with twin witches?

Answer: You can't tell which witch is which.

What rock group has four guys who don't sing?

Answer: Mount Rushmore.

What's a monster's favorite place to swim?

Answer: Lake Eerie.

What question can you never answer "yes" to?

Answer: Are you asleep?

Mr. Blue lives in the blue house, Mr. Pink lives in the pink house, and Mr. Brown lives in the brown house. Who lives in the white house?

Answer: The President.

Why do dogs run in circles?

Answer: Because it's too hard to run in squares.

What is the capital of Washington?

Answer: W.

What do you call a bear with no teeth?

Answer: A gummy bear.

Why did the Archaeopteryx catch the worm?

Answer: Because it was an early bird.

Why did the cow cross the road?

Answer: To get to the udder side.

How do you make the number one disappear?

Answer: Add the letter G and it's "GONE"

If a man was born in Greece, raised in Spain, came to America, and died in San Francisco, what is he?

Answer: Dead

What do you call a boomerang that doesn't return?

Answer: A stick.

Why do cows wear bells?

Answer: Their horns don't work.

What do prisoners use to call each other?

Answer: Cellphones.

Where was the Declaration of Independence signed?

Answer: At the bottom.

Why does a flamingo stand on one leg?

Answer: Because if he lifted that leg off the ground he would fall down.

What did the inventor of the door-knocker win?

Answer: The no-bell prize.

What nails do carpenters hate to hit?

Answer: Fingernails.

What goes through towns and over hills but never moves?

Answer: A Road

What's the greatest worldwide use of cowhide?

Answer: To hold cows together

What part of the car is the laziest?

Answer: The wheels, because they are always tired.

Two waves had a race. Who won?

Answer: They tide.

What's at the end of everything?

Answer: The letter "g".

I go around the yard but never move. What am I?

Answer: A fence

Why was the strawberry sad?

Answer: Because her mom was in a jam.

What do you get when dinosaurs crash their cars?

Answer: Tyrannosaurus wrecks.

What did the dinosaur say after the car crash?

Answer: I'm-so-saurus.

How do teddy bears keep their den cool in summer?

Answer: They use bear conditioning.

Where does a peacock go when it loses its tail?

Answer: A re-tail store.

Waiter, will my pizza be long?

Answer: No sir, it will be round.

How does the man-in-the-moon cut his hair?

Answer: Eclipse it.

You answer me, although I never ask you questions. What am I?

Answer: A telephone

What is always coming but never arrives?

Answer: Tomorrow

What can you hear but not touch or see?

Answer: Your voice.

Why didn't Cinderella make the basketball team?

Answer: She ran away from the ball.

Why did the baker stop making doughnuts?

Answer: She was bored with the hole business.

What loses its head in the morning but gets it back at night?

Answer: A pillow

What kind of plates do they use in space?

Answer: Flying saucers.

Why did the golfer have an extra pair of pants?

Answer: In case he got a hole in one.

What position does a ghost play in soccer?

Answer: Ghoulie.

Jack rode into town on Friday and rode out 2 days later on Friday. How can that be possible?

Answer: Friday is his horse's name!

What vegetables do librarians like?

Answer: Quiet peas.

What is the last thing you take off before bed?

Answer: Your feet off the floor.

Why did the picture go to jail?

Answer: Because it was framed.

What happened when the lion ate the clown?

Answer: He felt funny.

Did you hear about the origami store?

Answer: It folded.

Why is a tree like a big dog?

Answer: They both have lot of bark.

I have keys but no locks. I have space but no room. You can enter but can't go outside. What am I?

Answer: A Keyboard

If a crocodile makes shoes, what does a banana make?

Answer: Slippers.

What has a thumb and four fingers but is not alive?

Answer: A glove.

If two's company and three's a crowd, what are four and five?

Answer: Nine.

Why was everyone so tired on April 1st?

Answer: They had just finished a March of 31 days.

What did the computer do at lunchtime?

Answer: It had a byte.

Why did the cyclops stop teaching?

Answer: Because he only had one pupil.

What is the shortest month?

Answer: May, because it has only 3 letters.

If April showers bring May flowers, what do May flowers bring?

Answer: Pilgrims.

If the Pilgrims were alive today, what would they be most famous for?

Answer: Their age.

What gets wetter as it dries?

Answer: A towel.

What goes up and doesn't come back down?

Answer: Your age.

What subject in school is easy for a witch?

Answer: Spell-ing.

A woman has seven daughters, and each daughter has a brother. How many children does the woman have all together?

Answer: She has eight children.

What is harder to catch the faster you run?

Answer: Your breath.

What does the zero say to the eight?

Answer: Nice belt.

What type of bow cannot be tied?

Answer: A rain-bow.

What is the hardest part about skydiving?

Answer: The ground.

Why was the math book sad?

Answer: Because it had too many problems.

Where can you always find money?

Answer: In the dictionary.

What has one head, one foot and four legs?

Answer: A Bed

Why did Superman cross the road?

Answer: To get to the supermarket.

What do you call Tyrannosaurus rex when it wears a cowboy hat and boots?

Answer: Tyrannosaurus tex.

How many letters are in The Alphabet?

Answer: There are 11 letters in The Alphabet

What's worse than finding a worm in your apple?

Answer: Finding half a worm in your apple.

Why did the scarecrow win the Nobel Prize?

Answer: Because he was out standing in his field.

David's father had three sons: Snap, Crackle, and …?

Answer: David

What do witches put on their bagels?

Answer: Scream cheese.

What English word has three consecutive double letters?

Answer: Bookkeeper

What is full of holes but can still hold water?

Answer: A sponge.

What's green and smells like blue paint?

Answer: Green paint.

What is the coldest country in the world?

Answer: Chili.

Why is the mushroom always invited to parties?

Answer: Because he's a fungi.

How do trees get on the Internet?

Answer: They log in.

What day do potatoes hate the most?

Answer: Fry-day.

Where does success come before work?

Answer: In the dictionary.

Do you know how to make a witch itch?

Answer: You take away the w.

What breaks when you say it?

Answer: Silence.

Why did the teacher wear sunglasses?

Answer: Because her students were bright.

What kind of dinosaur can you ride in a rodeo?

Answer: A Bronco-saurus.

A cowboy rides into town on Friday, stays for three days, then leaves on Friday. How did he do it?

Answer: His horse's name was Friday.

What does a dentist call his X-rays?

Answer: Tooth-pics.

What did the nut say when it sneezed?

Answer: Cashew.

I have all the knowledge you have. But I am as small your fist that your hands can hold me. What am I?

Answer: I'm your brain

How does a witch tell time?

Answer: With a witch watch.

What's that gooey stuff in between a shark's teeth?

Answer: Slow swimmers.

Why is a piano so hard to open?

> *Answer: Because the keys are on the inside.*

Take off my skin - I won't cry, but you will. What am I?

> *Answer: an onion*

What only starts to work after it's fired?

> *Answer: A rocket.*

What do you call 150 strawberries bunched together?

> *Answer: A strawberry jam.*

What has one eye but cannot see?

> *Answer: a needle*

What do you call a man at the top of a hill?

> *Answer: Cliff.*

What's a great name for a lawyer?

> *Answer: Sue.*

What do you call a man in a hole?

> *Answer: Doug.*

What do you call a woman standing on a tennis court?

Answer: Annette.

What do you call a man lying on your doorstep?

Answer: Matt.

What do you call a man in the mailbox?

Answer: Bill.

What do you call a woman with one leg?

Answer: Aileen.

Who am I? I am the building with number stories.

Answer: A Library

The more you have of it, the less you see. What is it?

Darkness

Who won the skeleton beauty contest?

Answer: No body.

How do trains hear?

Answer: Through their engine-ears.

Each morning I appear to lie at your feet. All day I will follow no matter how fast you run, yet I nearly perish in the midday sun. What am I.

Answer: A shadow

What has a neck and no head, two arms but no hands?

Answer: A shirt

What is out of bounds?

Answer: A tired kangaroo.

What is the strongest creature in the sea?

Answer: A mussel.

Which type of dinosaur could jump higher than a house?

Answer: Any kind. A house can't jump.

What is put on a table, cut, but never eaten?

Answer: Cards

Why didn't the skeleton cross the road?

Answer: It didn't have the guts.

It cannot be seen, it weighs nothing, but when put into a barrel, it makes it lighter. What is it?

Answer: A hole

Why didn't the dinosaur cross the road?

Answer: There weren't any roads then.

What do you get if you cross a pig with a dinosaur?

Answer: Jurassic Pork.

Where do fish sleep?

Answer: On a seabed.

Lighter than what I am made of, more of me is hidden Than is seen.

Answer: An iceberg

What is the most slippery country in the world?

Answer: Greece

What do you call a dinosaur with one leg?

Answer: Eileen.

A man is pushing his car along the road when he comes to a hotel. He shouts, "I'm bankrupt!" Why?

Answer: He's playing monopoly

What do you call a sleeping bull?

Answer: A bull-dozer.

At night they come without being fetched. By day they are lost without being stolen. What are they?

Answer: The stars.

A box without hinges, lock or key, yet golden treasure lies within. What is it?

Answer: An egg

What makes a loud noise when changing its jacket, becomes larger but weighs less?

Answer: Popcorn

What has a foot but no legs?

Answer: A snail

Where do baby ghosts go during the day?

Answer: Dayscare.

Who earns a living by driving their customers away?

Answer: A taxi driver.

What comes down but never goes up?

Answer: Rain

What building has the most stories?

Answer: The library.

What's a tornado's favorite game?

Answer: Twister.

Why do dinosaurs eat raw meat?

Answer: Because they don't know how to cook.

Why is there a gate around cemeteries?

Answer: Because people are dying to get in.

What did dinosaurs have that no others animals ever had?

Answer: Baby dinosaurs.

What did the duck say after he went shopping?

Answer: Put it on my bill.

How do you stop an elephant from charging?

Answer: Take away her credit card.

Mary's father has 5 daughters – Nana, Nene, Nini, Nono. What is the fifth daughter's name?

Answer: Mary

Why are movie stars always cool?

Answer: Because they have so many fans.

Why did the woman run around her bed?

Answer: She wanted to catch up on her sleep.

What word becomes shorter when you add two letters to it?

Answer: Short

What occurs once in a minute, twice in a moment and never in one thousand years?

Answer: The letter M

If I have it, I don't share it. If I share it, I don't have it. What is it?

Answer: A Secret.

What can you catch but not throw?

Answer: A cold.

A house has 4 walls. All of the walls are facing south, and a bear is circling the house. What color is the bear?

Answer: The house is on the north pole, so the bear is white.

What is as light as a feather, but even the world's strongest man couldn't hold it for more than a minute?

Answer: His breath.

What snakes are good at doing sums?

Answer: Adders.

What do you call a camel with no humps?

Answer:Humphrey.

What's the key to a great Thanksgiving dinner?

Answer: The turkey.

You walk into a room with a match, a kerosene lamp, a candle, and a fireplace. Which do you light first?

A: The match.

We see it once in a year, twice in a week, and never in a day. What is it?

Answer: The letter "E"

What does a sick lemon need?

Answer: Lemon aid.

What goes up but never comes down?

Answer: Your age.

What gets broken without being held?

Answer: A promise

What is even smarter than a talking bird?

Answer: A spelling bee.

What has Eighty-eight keys but can't open a single door?

Answer: A piano

What has a head but never weeps, has a bed but never sleeps, can run but never walks, and has a bank but no money?

Answer: A river.

What's black and white and red all over?

Answer: A newspaper.

What do you call a grumpy cow?

Answer: Moo-dy

What has no fingers, but many rings?

Answer: A tree.

What happens when you throw a white hat into the Black Sea?

Answer: It gets wet.

Why do hummingbirds hum?

Answer: Because they forgot the words.

What did the dog say when he sat on sandpaper?

Answer: Ruff

What kind of hair do oceans have?

Answer: Wavy.

What has a bottom at the top?

Answer: Your legs.

Two fathers and two sons go on a fishing trip. They each catch a fish and bring it home. Why do they only bring 3 home?

Answer: The fishing trip consists of a grandfather, a father and a son.

What do you give a sick bird?

Answer: Tweetment.

The more it dries, the wetter it becomes. What is it?

Answer: A towel.

What do fish and maps have in common?

Answer: They both have scales.

What do you get when you cross a frog and a bunny?

Answer: A ribbit.

Which witch is good when it's dark?

Answer: A lights-witch.

Only two backbones and thousands of ribs.

Answer: A railroad

What did one flea say to the other?

Answer: Should we walk or take a dog?

What gives you the power and strength to walk through walls?

Answer: A door.

What's green and sings?

Answer: Elvis Parsley.

What did one wall say to the other wall?

Answer: I'll meet you at the corner.

What is something you will never see again?

Answer: Yesterday

A man was cleaning the windows of a 25 story building. He slipped and fell off the ladder, but wasn't hurt. How did he do it?

Answer: He fell off the 2nd step.

When is a car like a frog?

Answer: When it's being toad.

Why was the result when a piano fell down a mine shaft?

Answer: A-flat minor.

Four men sat down to play, and played all night till the break of day. They played for cash and not for fun, and had a separate score for every one. When it came time to square accounts they had all made money. How?

Answer: They were a dance band

Why do birds fly south for the winter?

Answer: Because it's too far to walk.

What do you call a cow that plays a musical instrument?

Answer: A Moo-sician.

What's the biggest problem with snow boots?

Answer: They melt.

Where can you find an ocean with no water?

Answer: On a map.

What has a face and two hands but no arms or legs?

Answer: A clock.

What washes up on very small beaches?

Answer: Microwaves.

What do you get if you cross a centipede and a parrot?

Answer: A walkie-talkie.

What has to be broken before you can use it?

Answer: An egg.

What kind of bird can carry the most weight?

Answer: The crane.

How do fleas travel from place to place?

Answer: By itch-hiking.

What can go up and come down without moving?

Answer: The temperature

What is an insect's favorite sport?

Answer: Cricket

What's noisier than a whooping crane?

Answer: A trumpeting swan

What has a neck but no head?

Answer: A bottle

Which month has 28 days?

Answer: All of them of course

Which side of a parrot has the prettiest feathers?

Answer: The outside.

If you were in a race and passed the person in 2nd place, what place would you be in?

Answer: 2nd place.

Why do male deer need braces?

Answer: Because they have buck teeth.

What's worse than raining cats and dogs?

Answer: Hailing taxis.

Why did the clown go to the doctor?

Answer: Because he was feeling a little funny.

Why did the kid throw the butter out the window?

Answer: To see the butter fly.

What's orange and sounds like a parrot?

Answer: A carrot.

What has a head, a tail, is brown, and has no legs?

Answer: A penny.

Where does Dracula keep his money?

Answer: In a blood bank.

How many books can you put into an empty backpack?

Answer: One. After that it's not empty.

Two silk worms were in a race. Who won?

Answer: It was a tie.

Which fish is the most famous?

Answer: The star fish.

What do you get when you cross a shark and a snowman?

Answer: Frostbite.

What do you get if you cross a dog and an airplane?

Answer: A jet setter.

What is the biggest ant in the world?

Answer: An eleph-ant.

Jack and Jill are lying on the floor inside the house, dead. They died from lack of water. There is shattered glass next to them. How did they die?

Answer: Jack and Jill are goldfish.

What breed of dog does Dracula have?

Answer: A bloodhound.

What geometric figure is like a lost parrot?

Answer: A polygon.

What do you get when you cross an elephant and a fish?

Answer: Swimming trunks.

As I walked along the path I saw something with four fingers and one thumb, but it was not flesh, fish, bone, or fowl.

Answer: A glove

Why don't lobsters share?

Answer: They are shellfish

Does your shirt have holes in it?

Answer: No, then how did you put it on?

What do you get if you cross a canary and a 50-foot long snake?

Answer: A sing-a-long

What do you get when you cross a snake and a pie?

Answer: A pie-thon.

A barrel of water weighs 20 pounds. What must you add to it to make it weigh 12 pounds?

Answer: Holes

A boy was rushed to the hospital emergency room. The ER doctor saw the boy and said, "I cannot operate on this boy. He is my son." But the doctor was not the boy's father. How could that be?

Answer: The doctor was his mother.

What animals are the best pets?

Answer: Cats, because they are purr-fect.

What was stolen from the music store?

Answer: The lute.

I am an odd number. Take away one letter and I become even. What number am I?

Answer: Seven (take away the 's' and it becomes 'even').

What never asks questions but is often answered?

Answer: A doorbell.

When you look for something, why is it always in the last place you look?

Answer: Because when you find it, you stop looking.

Martha Martin was born on December 27th, yet her birthday is always in the summer. How is this possible?

Answer: She lives in the Southern Hemisphere

What kind of coat can only be put on when wet?

Answer: A coat of paint.

What did the cat have for breakfast?

Answer: Mice Crispies.

What do you serve that you can't eat?

Answer: A tennis ball.

I have rivers, but don't have water. I have dense forests, but no trees and animals. I have cities, but no people live in those cities. What am I?

Answer: A map

I have no life, but I can die, what am I?

Answer: A battery

I'm tall when I'm young and I'm short when I'm old. What am I?

Answer: A candle

If a rooster laid a brown egg and a white egg, what kind of chicks would hatch?

Answer: A rooster doesn't lay eggs

He has married many women but has never married. Who is he?

Answer: A priest

What has 4 eyes but can't see?

Answer: Mississippi

What do you get if you cross Bambi with a ghost?

Answer: Bamboo.

What do you fill with empty hands?

Answer: Gloves

Why did the lion spit out the clown?

Answer: Because he tasted funny.

Take away my first letter, and I still sound the same. Take away my last letter, I still sound the same. Even take away my letter in the middle, I will still sound the same. I am a five letter word. What am I?

Answer: Empty

What is at the end of a rainbow?

Answer: The letter W.

What do you call a deer with no eyes?

Answer: No idea

What do you call a deer with no eyes and no legs?

Answer: Still no idea.

What animal is bad to play games with?

Answer: A cheetah.

What starts with the letter "t", is filled with "t" and ends in "t"?

Answer: A teapot.

Which is correct to say, "The yolk of the egg are white?" or "The yolk of the egg is white?"

Answer: Neither, egg yolks are yellow

What is a frog's favorite music?

Answer: Hip hop.

What book was once owned by only the wealthy, but now everyone can have it? You can't buy it in a bookstore or take it from the library.

Answer: The telephone book

What is so delicate that saying its name breaks it?

Answer: Silence.

What do you call a sleeping dinosaur?

Answer: A dino-snore.

Why did the leopard wear a striped shirt?

Answer: So she wouldn't be spotted.

A man was driving his truck. His lights were not on. The moon was not out. Up ahead, a woman was crossing the street. How did he see her?

Answer: It was a bright and sunny day.

They come out at night without being called, and are lost in the day without being stolen. What are they?

Answer: Stars

A monkey, a squirrel, and a bird are racing to the top of a coconut tree. Who will get the banana first, the monkey, the squirrel, or the bird?

Answer: None of them, because you can't get a banana from a coconut tree.

When is it very bad luck to see a black cat?

Answer: When you're a mouse.

What is the easiest way to double your money?

Answer: Put it in front of the mirror.

Is it hard to spot a leopard?

Answer: No, they come that way

Everyone has it and no one can lose it, what is it?

Answer: A shadow.

What belongs to you but other people use it more than you?

Answer: Your name.

The more you take, the more you leave behind. What are they?

Answer: Footprints.

You will throw me away when you want to use me. You will take me in when you don't want to use me. What am I?

Answer: An anchor

What sort of steps do you take if you a tiger is running towards you?

Answer: Big ones.

I will always come, never arrive today. What am I?

Answer: Tomorrow

If you give me water, I will die. What am I?

Answer: A fire

Where do tough chickens come from?

Answer: Hard-boiled eggs.

I don't speak, can't hear or speak anything, but I will always tell the truth. What am I?

Answer: A mirror

Why did the chicken cross the road?

Answer: To get to the other side.

Why did the chewing gum cross the road?

Answer: It was stuck to the chicken's foot.

Why did the turkey cross the road?

Answer: It was the chicken's day off.

Why did the turkey cross the road twice?

Answer: To prove he wasn't chicken.

I run, yet I have no legs. What am I?

Answer: A nose

What kind of room has no windows or doors?

Answer: A mushroom

Take one out and scratch my head, I am now black but once was red.

Answer: A match

I look at you, you look at me, I raise my right, you raise your left. What is this object?

Answer: A mirror

What do you call it when it rains chickens and ducks?

Answer: Fowl weather.

What goes around the world and stays in a corner?

Answer: A stamp

It has no top or bottom but it can hold flesh, bones, and blood all at the same time. What is this object?

Answer: A ring

Which side of a chicken has the most feathers?

Answer: The outside

The more there is, the less you see.

Answer: Darkness

What must we do before we can have our sins forgiven?

Answer: Sin

What has 12 legs, six eyes, three tails, and can't see?

Answer: Three blind mice.

It has a golden head

It has a golden tail

but it has no body.

Answer: Gold coin

Runs smoother than any rhyme,

loves to fall but cannot climb!

Answer: water

Why can't a rooster ever get rich?

Answer: Because he works for chicken feed.

I am in the center of Paris, at the end of the Eiffel Tower and I start every race.

Answer: The letter R

I'm where yesterday follows today,

And tomorrow is in the middle.

Answer: A dictionary

What's the most musical part of a chicken?

Answer: The drumstick

I am black when you buy me, red when you use me, and grey when you throw me away.

Answer: Coal

What is it that, after you take away the whole, some still remains?

Answer: The word wholesome

Why did the chicken go to the séance?

Answer: To get to the other side.

Whoever makes it, tells it not.

Whoever takes it, knows it not.

Whoever knows it, wants it not.

Answer: Counterfeit money

Made in the USA
San Bernardino, CA
11 May 2020